Reflections by ROSA PARKS

The Quiet Strength and Faith of a

Woman Who Changed a Nation

Reflections by
ROSA PARKS

ROSA PARKS **with** Gregory J. Reed

Previously published as *Quiet Strength*

ZONDERVAN

Reflections by Rosa Parks
Copyright © 1994 by Rosa L. Parks
Previously published as *Quiet Strength*

Requests for information should be addressed to:
Zondervan, *3900 Sparks Dr. SE, Grand Rapids, Michigan 49546*

ISBN 978-0-310-35156-6 (hardcover)
ISBN 978-0-310-35310-2 (audio)
ISBN 978-0-310-35157-3 (ebook)

Epilogue from *Resurrection of Rosa Parks: The Branding of Icon, Spirit and Soul* by Gregory J. Reed.
Copyright © 2006 by Gregory J. Reed. Reprinted by permission of Keeper of the Word Foundation.

Library of Congress Cataloging-in-Publication Data

Parks, Rosa, 1913–2005
    Quiet strength: the faith, the hope, and the heart of a woman who changed a nation / Rosa Parks with
  Gregory J. Reed.
      p. cm.
    Includes bibliographical references.
    ISBN: 0-310-50150-4 (hardcover: alk. paper)
    1. Parks, Rosa, 1913–. 2. Afro-Americans—Alabama—Montgomery—Biography. 3. Civil rights
  workers—Alabama—Montgomery—Biography. 4. Segregation in transportation—Alabama—
  Montgomery—History—20th century. I. Reed, Gregory J. II. Title.
  F334.M79P37 1994
  323'.092—dc20 94—46141
  [B] CIP

Cover design: Curt Diepenhorst
Cover photo: Paul Schutzer/Getty Images
Interior design: Denise Froehlich

Edited by Verne Becker and Elaine Steele

First printing November 2017 / Printed in the United States of America

In memory of my great-grandmother Jane and great-grandpa James Percival, grandparents Rose and John Edwards, mother Leona Edwards McCauley, brother Sylvester McCauley, husband Raymond Parks

—ROSA L. PARKS

With love to my daughters Arian and Ashley, and sister Sharon Lawson, and brother Narraine Reed for their inspiration and support. To my mother Bertha and my adopted mothers Maureen Pearson and Alma Whitley for the love and guidance they have given me throughout my life. I thank them for being excellent role models. And finally, to my grandmothers Zemine Wourman

—GREGORY J. REED

Contents

Acknowledgments

T o Elaine Steele, dearest friend, and Gregory J. Reed, who have been a source of strength and support in my life. I am grateful for their many contributions, including the technical editing of this book by Elaine Steele.

—ROSA L. PARKS

The coauthor gratefully acknowledges Elaine Steele, the cofounder of the Rosa and Raymond Parks Institute for Self-Development. Her support and guidance have helped make it possible to expand the legacy of Rosa Parks so that others can learn from her life and words.

A special thanks to Stan Gundry of Zondervan, and Kelli Monteiro, the primary researcher, analyzer, and organizer, who made striking comments that helped establish the infrastructure for the text of this book. To Dr. Otis Stanley, a key contributor, for his patience, ideas, and suggestions, which were invaluable in improving the *Quiet Strength* book. Also, to my dear friends, protectors of the Parks Legacy: Dr. C. Eric Lincoln, Richard

Manson, Stephanie L. Hammonds, Maurita Coley, Johnnie L. Cochran, Pres. Barrack Obama, Nelson Mandela, Alex Haley, Joe Madison, Muhammad Ali, Deepak Chopra, Coretta Scott King, Oprah Winfrey, Virginia Durr, Johnnie Carr, Dr. Charles Wright, Antoinette Wright, Malik Shabazz, Dr. Glenda Curry, Hon. John Conyers, Julia Carson, JoAnn Watson, Brenda Jones, Don Davis, Beryl Anderson, Carl R. Edwards Esq., O'Neil and Linda Swanson, Dr. Linda Lott, Khalid el-Hakim, Dr. Robert Green, Coleman A. Young, Robert Millender, Jack Boland, Douglas Brinkley, William Harris, William C. and Betty Brooks, Derrick A. Humphries, David Ashenfelder, Tavis Smiley, Cornel West, and Mildred Gaddis.

And thanks to supporters of the Legacy: Dr. Curtis Ivery, Munson Steed, Hon. Christopher Brown, Kenneth Watson, Damon Flournoy, Paul Katz, Rod Spencer, Jeff Wardford, Robert Wourman, Blane Hailemichael, Jayron Jenkins, Herb Boyd, Nikki Howard Combs, Karen Lloyd, Marie Christmon, Cherron Jones, Kwame Kenyatta, Marcel Todd, Dr. James Blessman, Perri Keys, Steven Reifman Esq., BESLA Founders, Morris Jenkins, Keeper of the Word Foundation, and Million Man March ... and countless others, for their courage and bravery.

—GREGORY J. REED

About Rosa Parks

Rosa Louise Parks is nationally recognized as the mother of the modern-day civil rights movement in America. By refusing to surrender her seat to a white male passenger on a Montgomery, Alabama, bus on December 1, 1955, she set in motion a chain of events that were felt throughout the United States. Her quiet, courageous act changed America and redirected the course of history.

She was born Rosa Louise McCauley on February 4, 1913, in Tuskegee, Alabama. She was the first child of James and Leona (Edwards) McCauley. Several years later her family moved to Pine Level, Alabama, where she was educated in a rural schoolhouse.

When Rosa completed her education in Pine Level at age eleven, her mother enrolled her in Montgomery Industrial School for Girls (also known as Miss White's School for Girls), a private institution. Several years later she went on to Alabama State Teachers' College for Negroes for tenth and eleventh grade. She was unable to graduate with her class, however, because of the illness and subsequent death of her grandmother, Rose Edwards. As Rosa prepared to return to school, her mother also became ill, so she remained home to care for her mother while her younger brother, Sylvester, worked to help support the family.

Rosa married Raymond Parks on December 18, 1932. Raymond was born in Wedowee, Alabama, in 1903. He received little formal education because of racial segregation; but with the encouragement of his mother, Geri Parks, Raymond educated himself. As an adult, his thorough knowledge of domestic affairs and current events led most people to believe he had gone to college. He supported Rosa's desire to complete her formal education, and in 1934 she received her high school diploma.

Raymond was an early activist in the effort to free the Scottsboro Boys, a highly-publicized case in the 1930s. Together Raymond and Rosa worked in the National Association for the Advancement of Colored People (NAACP). He was an active member, and she served as secretary and, later, as youth leader of the local Montgomery branch. At the time of her arrest, she was preparing for a major youth conference.

Four days after her arrest, the black people of Montgomery and sympathizers of other races organized and promoted a boycott of the city bus line. For 381 days, blacks either walked or arranged their own rides throughout the city rather than taking the bus. Reverend Martin Luther King Jr., the appointed spokesperson for the boycott, emphasized the importance of nonviolence by all participants. Following the lead of Montgomery, other protests took shape throughout the country—sit-ins, eat-ins, swim-ins, and more. Thousands of courageous people joined together to demand equal rights for all. The bus boycott ended on December 21, 1956, after the U.S. Supreme Court declared bus segregation unconstitutional.

Mr. and Mrs. Parks moved to Detroit in 1957, and she remained active in the civil rights movement: traveling, speaking, and participating in peaceful demonstrations. From 1965 to 1988 Rosa worked in the office of Congressman John Conyers of Michigan. Her husband died in 1977, and in 1987 she began the Rosa and Raymond Parks Institute for Self-Development. Its purpose is to motivate and direct youth to achieve their highest potential. Rosa saw the energy of young people as a real force for change. It was among her most treasured themes as she spoke at schools, colleges, and national organizations around the country.

An example of quiet courage, dignity, and determination, Rosa Parks is a symbol of freedom for the world.

Fear

Yea, though I walk through the valley of the shadow of death, I will fear no evil: for thou art with me.

—PSALM 23:4

(Archives/UIG/REX/Shutterstock)

Rosa Parks sitting on a bus in Montgomery, December 21, 1956, on the day the city buses were legally integrated.

As a child, I learned from the Bible to trust in God and not be afraid. I have always felt comforted by reading the Psalms, especially Psalms 23 and 27.

My grandfather also influenced me to not be afraid. A very proud man, he was never fearful—especially when it came to defending his home and family. Back in those days, fear was something very real for black people. There was so much hatred toward blacks—especially from white supremacy groups, like the Ku Klux Klan.

I remember one day when the KKK came near our house after many incidents of hate crimes against nearby blacks. My grandfather never seemed afraid. At night he would sit with his shotgun and say that he did not know how long he would last, but if they came breaking in our house, he was going to get the first one who came through the door. He never looked for trouble, but he believed in defending his home.

I saw and heard so much as a child growing up with hate and injustice against black people. I learned to put my trust in God and to seek Him as my strength. Long ago I set my mind to be a free person and not to give in to fear. I always felt that it was my right to defend myself if I could.

I have learned over the years that when one's mind is made up, this diminishes fear; knowing what must be done does away with fear. When I sat down on the bus the day I was arrested, I was thinking of going home. I had made up my mind quickly about what it was that I had to do, what I felt was right to do. I did not think of being physically tired or fearful. After so many years of oppression and being a victim of the mistreatment that my people had suffered, not giving up my seat—and whatever I had to face after not giving it up—was not important. I did not feel any fear at sitting in the seat I was sitting in. All I felt was tired. Tired of being pushed around. Tired of seeing the bad treatment and disrespect of children, women, and men just because of the color of their skin. Tired of the Jim Crow laws. Tired of being oppressed. I was just plain tired.

I felt the Lord would give me the strength to endure whatever I had to face. God did away with all my fear. It was time for someone to stand up—or in my case, sit down. I refused to move.

We blacks are not as fearful or divided as people may think. I cannot let myself be so afraid that I am unable to move around freely and express myself. If I do, then I am undoing the gains we have made in the civil rights movement. Love, not fear, must be our guide.

In these days, many people are feeling a different type of fear that is hard to break free of. There are so many new things to be afraid of that were not as common in the earlier days. We should not let fear overcome us. We must remain strong. Violence and crime seem so much more prevalent. It is easy to say that we have come a long way, but we still have a long way to go. Many of our children are going astray. But I still remain hopeful.

Defiance

The last shall be first, and the first last.
—MATTHEW 20:16

Rosa Parks with her attorney, Charles D. Langford, on her way to jail
for helping to organize a citywide bus boycott, February 22, 1956.

After the 1954 Supreme Court ruling on *Brown v. Board of Education*, which designated separate-but-equal schools for children unlawful, a few people felt optimistic that things would get better. The laws were changed, but the heart of America remained unchanged.

One day I noticed a little child whose mother was taking him to one of the integrated schools. From the nervous look on his face I could tell he did not want to go to that white school, and his mother, she did not know what was going to happen. It was not easy for a small child to walk into a place of merely token integration, where a multitude of white persons had always been taught there should be racial segregation.

Despite the banning of separate schools for the races, most people did not react too favorably. They were more indifferent than interested. It was not easy, you see, because the pattern had existed so long. There were still separate elevators and fountains for white and colored people. I used them as little as possible.

The more I became involved with the NAACP, the more I learned of discrimination and acts of violence against blacks, such as lynchings, rapes, and unsolved murders. And the more I learned about these incidents, the more I felt I could no longer passively sit by and accept the Jim Crow laws. A better day had to come.

The custom for getting on the bus for black persons in Montgomery in 1955 was to pay at the front door, get off the bus, and then re-enter through the back door to find a seat. On the buses, if white persons got on, the colored would move back if the white section was filled. Black people could not sit in the same row with white people. They could not even sit across the aisle from each other. Some customs were humiliating, and this one was intolerable since we were the majority of the ridership.

On Thursday evening, December 1, I was riding the bus home from work. A white man got on, and the driver looked our way and said, "Let me have those seats." It did not seem proper, particularly for a woman to give her seat to a man. All the passengers paid ten cents, just as he did. When more whites boarded the bus, the driver, J. P. Blake, ordered the blacks in the fifth row, the first row of the colored section (the row I was sitting in), to move to the rear. Bus drivers then had police powers, under both municipal and state laws, to enforce racial segregation. However, we were sitting in the section designated for colored.

At first none of us moved.

"Y'all better make it light on yourselves and let me have those seats," Blake said.

Then three of the blacks in my row got up, but I stayed in my seat and slid closer to the window. I do not remember being frightened. But I sure did not believe I would "make it light" on myself by standing up. Our mistreatment was just not right, and I was tired of it. The more we gave in, the worse they treated us. I kept thinking about my mother and my grandparents, and how strong they were. I knew there was a possibility of being mistreated, but an opportunity was being given to me to do what I had asked of others.

I knew someone had to take the first step. So I made up my mind not to move. Blake asked me if I was going to stand up.

"No. I am not," I answered.

Blake said that he would have to call the police. I said, "Go ahead." In less than five minutes, two policemen came, and the driver pointed me out. He said that he wanted the seat and that I would not stand up.

"Why do you push us around?" I said to one of the policemen.

"I don't know," he answered, "but the law is the law and you're under arrest."

I did not get on the bus to get arrested; I got on the bus to go home. Getting arrested was one of the worst days in my life. It was not a happy experience. Since I have always been a strong believer in God, I knew that He was with me, and only He could get me through the next step.

I had no idea that history was being made. I was just tired of giving in. Somehow, I felt that what I did was right by standing up to that bus driver. I did not think about the consequences. I knew that I could have been lynched, manhandled, or beaten when the police came. I chose not to move. When I made that decision, I knew that I had the strength of my ancestors with me.

There were other people on the bus whom I knew. But when I was arrested, not one of them came to my defense. I felt very much alone. One man who knew me did not even go by my house to tell my husband I had been arrested. Everyone just went on their way.

In jail I felt even more alone. For a moment, as I sat in that little room with bars, before I was moved to a cell with two other women, I felt that I had been deserted. But I did not cry. I said a silent prayer and waited.

Later that evening, to my great relief, I was released. It is strange: after the arrest, I never did reach the breaking point of shedding tears. The next day, I returned to work. It was pouring down rain, so I called a cab. The young man at work was so surprised to see me. He thought I would be too nervous and shaken to go back to work.

Three days later I was found guilty and ordered to pay a ten-dollar fine plus four dollars in court costs. The case was later appealed with the help of one of my attorneys, Fred Gray, and I did not have to pay anything.

It is funny to me how people came to believe that the reason that I did not move from my seat was that my feet were tired. I did not hear this until I moved to Detroit in 1957. My feet were not tired, but *I* was tired—tired of unfair treatment. I also heard later that Mother Pollard, one of the marchers in Montgomery, said that my feet were tired but my soul was rested. She was right about my soul.

On Monday, December 5, the day I went to court, the Montgomery Improvement Association (MIA) was formed to start the bus boycott. It is sad, in a way, to think about what we had to go through to get to that point. We, as a people, all felt discouraged with our situation, but we had not been united enough to conquer it. Now, the fearfulness and bitterness was turning into power.

So the people started organizing, protesting, and walking. Many thousands were willing to sacrifice the comfort and convenience of riding the bus. This was the modern mass movement we needed. I suppose they were showing sympathy for a person who had been mistreated. It was not just my arrest that year. Many African-Americans, including Emmet Till, had been killed or beaten for racist reasons. I was the third woman in Montgomery to be arrested on a bus. We reached the point where we simply had to take action.

Nearly a year later the segregated-bus ordinance was declared unconstitutional by the U.S. Supreme Court. One day after the boycott ended, I rode a nonsegregated bus for the first time.

A month after the boycott began, I lost my twenty-five-dollar-a-week job when the now-defunct Montgomery Fair department store closed its tailor shop. I was given no indication from the store that my boycott activities were the reason I lost my job. People always wanted to say it was because of my involvement in the boycott. I cannot say this is true. I do not like to form in my mind something I do not have any proof of.

Four decades later I am still uncomfortable with the credit given to me for starting the bus boycott. Many people do not know the whole truth; I would like them to know I was not the only person involved. I was just one of many who fought for freedom. And many others around me began to *want* to fight for their rights as well.

At that time, the Reverend Martin Luther King Jr. was emerging on the scene. He once said, "If you will protest courageously and yet with dignity and Christian love, when the history books are written in future generations, the historians will have to pause and say: there lived a great people—a black people—who injected new meaning and dignity into the veins of civilization." It was these words that guided many of us as we faced the trials and tribulations of fighting for our rights.

Injustice

Judge not according to the appearance, but judge righteous judgment.

—JOHN 7:24

Rosa Parks being fingerprinted in Montgomery, Alabama, after her arrest on anti-boycott charges, February 22, 1956. Ninety-one other people were arrested.

I am always troubled whenever I see injustice against any race of people. Growing up in the South, I saw so much of this that I feel deeply that no human being should ever be treated unjustly. I am concerned about any discrimination, of any people, regardless of race or other physical differences. We are all God's children and deserving of His rewards.

Before the Supreme Court ruled that bus segregation was illegal, black people were forced to pay their fares at the front, then get off the bus and walk around to the side door to get to the back-seats. Sometimes, before these paid passengers reached the other door, the bus drivers would drive off. It always amazed me that people would go along with this practice. It seemed natural to me to want to be treated as a human being. The Jim Crow bus system in Montgomery at that time was offensive to me.

The civil rights movement was closely tied to the church in its fight against injustice. People often ask me, "Why was the church a part of the movement?" It was the only legal place our people could gather and get information without being harassed or unjustly treated. We could not depend on the newspaper for accurate information. The church was and is the foundation of our community. It became our strength, our refuge, and our haven. We would pray, sing, and meet in church. We would use Scriptures, testimonies, and hymns to strengthen us against all the hatred and violence going on around us.

Most black churches worked in the struggle to overcome racial discrimination. They identified with the Exodus in the Old Testament, and God's concern for freeing his people. In the early days, churches often helped hide slaves who were trying to escape to freedom. Members of the church would risk their lives to help these people. The church has always been a part of helping others.

Many of us, and particularly young people, need to study our history to understand the foundations of our movement. That is why I started the "Pathways to Freedom" program, one of the programs of the Rosa and Raymond Parks Institute for Self-Development, which traces the underground railroad into the civil rights movement and beyond. It teaches our youth about their history and provides a sense of pride in who they are and where they have come from.

I have been a member of the African Methodist Episcopal (A.M.E.) church all of my life. My father's brother-in-law was pastor of the A.M.E. church in Pine Level, Alabama. The denomination became known as "The Freedom Church" during the abolitionist movement. It was the spiritual home of many well-known black persons in our history before civil rights. They include Bishop Richard Allen (the founder of the A.M.E. church), Frederick Douglass, Harriet Tubman, Sojourner Truth, and others. They all were strongly rooted in the A.M.E. church.

As long as people use tactics to oppress or restrict other people from being free, there is work to be done. Although we have made many gains, racism is still alive. A few years back, the city of Dearborn, Michigan, an area that is predominantly white, passed an ordinance restricting most of its parks to "residents only." It seemed odd that they would discourage our presence in their parks while welcoming our dollars in their stores.

That ordinance in Dearborn was like many of the intimidating tactics we had to fight against in the civil rights movement. Of course, Dearborn in 1985 was not Montgomery in 1955. However, the same kind of protest tactics were effective. What we had to put up with in the South in those days was so awful that I could not bear to see it happening again.

Pain

It is commendable if someone bears up under the pain of unjust suffering because they are conscious of God.

—1 PETER 2:19 NIV

Rosa Parks being escorted up the courthouse steps by E. D. Nixon, President of the Alabama NAACP, March 19, 1956.

On Tuesday evening, August 31, 1994, I heard a loud noise. When I went downstairs to see what it was, I saw a young black male standing in my living room. I was startled.

"Someone knocked down your door," he said, "but I chased him away. I'm here to protect you." Then he asked for three dollars.

I told him the money was upstairs, and as I went up to my room, he followed me. I felt uneasy, but I still did not fear for my life.

When I tried to give him the three dollars from my pocket, he asked for more. Then he started pushing me and striking me in the face. I tried to defend myself and grabbed his shirt. Even at eighty-one years of age, I felt it was my right to defend myself. The man said, "You're going to make me hurt you if you don't give me all your money." I had never been hit in that manner in my life. I screamed, but no one heard me. I gave him all that I had ($103), and then he left. He could have hurt me much worse, but God protected me.

I pray for this young man and the conditions in our country that have made him this way. I urge people not to read too much into the attack. I regret that some people, regardless of race, are in such a mental state that they would want to harm an older person. Young people need to be taught to respect and care for their elders. Despite the violence and crime in our society, we should not let fear overwhelm us. We must remain strong. We must not give up hope; we can overcome.

I experience problems and pain just like everyone else. I have learned throughout my life that what really matters is not whether we have problems but how we go through them. We must keep on going to make it through whatever we are facing.

Many people cannot relate to the feelings of frustration that we, as black people, felt in the 1950s. We were born and raised in America but were treated as second-class citizens. For many years black people accepted the treatment. I always felt it was unjust. But because we went along with it then did not mean that we would let it go on forever. It came a time when we would no longer tolerate it. It came a time when we just had to say enough was enough. It was a long time coming, but finally, as a group, we demanded, "Let my people go."

When we stood, we stood for all of the oppressed people who came before us and for generations to come. I was fortunate. God provided me with the strength I needed at the precise time when conditions were ripe for change. I am thankful to Him every day that He gave me the strength not to move. Not only did the civil rights movement help our people, but it set a model for people fighting for freedom around the world.

It has always been very difficult, very painful, to think about Dr. Martin Luther King's death. He was a very dear friend of mine. His faith, his words, and his commitment to nonviolence inspired all of us in the civil rights movement. When a woman stabbed him in New York in 1958, I was terribly shocked. It was a rude awakening to realize that he had to face this kind of danger every day. Ten years later when he was assassinated, I was no longer surprised that it could happen, but I was still deeply grieved. Mama and I had been listening to a minister on the radio when the newscaster broke in and announced that Dr. King had been shot. We were deeply hurt, and we wept in each other's arms.

We, as a race of people, should learn to work more closely together. During the Montgomery bus boycott, we came together and remained unified for 381 days. It has never been done again. The Montgomery boycott became the model for human rights throughout the world. We must learn from the past. The gains we made came about because blacks realized that it takes cooperation and determination to make progress in their struggle toward equality. Today, in some ways, we are divided. If we could concentrate on one or two causes that most people can benefit from, it would be better. For certain causes, we are one—for others, we are not. We must learn to work together. No one can effectively fight for justice alone.

Things have improved for blacks since the 1955 boycott, but we are still being treated unequally. Many subtle customs and practices continue to discourage minorities and make them feel they do not have their place in a free society. Until everyone can enjoy the same opportunities, people cannot be equal. I am glad that segregation is no longer considered acceptable, but the fight for equal rights must go on until we have the same privileges and opportunities as those who are in power.

Character

All the people of my town know that you are a woman of noble character.

—RUTH 3:11 NIV

(Used by permission of AP/Wide World Photos)

Rosa Parks receiving an award, October 1986.

If you want to be respected for your actions, then your behavior must be above reproach. I learned from my grandmother and mother that one should always respect oneself and live right. This is how you gain the respect of others. If our lives demonstrate that we are peaceful, humble, and trusted, this is recognized by others. If our lives demonstrate something else, that will be noticed too.

From my upbringing and the Bible, I learned people should stand up for their rights, just as the children of Israel stood up to Pharaoh. When I reflect on conditions in the South, I recall that people had become worn out from being humiliated. They were sick of accepting the racial segregation that seemed to be worsening each day. Someone had to take that first step. In that moment on the bus, I decided to resist and take the consequences. It was worth it. I am glad to know that this and many other incidents have brought change.

Human dignity must be respected at all times. I would have

compromised my dignity if I had buckled one more time to the white establishment and relinquished my seat. The mistreatment would have continued. I also would have compromised my dignity if I had resisted violently.

Not standing up on the bus that night was a matter of self-respect. Every day of my life, I have wanted to be treated with respect, and I have wanted to treat others with respect. I had expected and hoped that others would feel the same. But because of my race, I was denied that respect. In many ways, that still happens among us today.

I find that if I am thinking too much of my own problems and the fact that at times things are not just like I want them to be, I do not make any progress at all. But if I look around and see what I can do, and then I do it, I move on.

In our struggle, if we are to bring about the kind of changes that will cause the world to stand up and take notice, we must be committed. There is so much work that needs to be done.

Every home and neighborhood in this country needs to be a safe, warm, and healthy place—a place fit for human beings as citizens of the United States. It is a big job, but there is no one better to do it than those who live here. Goodness and change are possible in each and every American citizen. We could show the world how it should be done and how to do it with dignity.

Role Models

In everything set them an example by doing what is good. In your teaching show integrity, seriousness and soundness of speech that cannot be condemned, so that those who oppose you may be ashamed because they have nothing bad to say about us.

—TITUS 2:7–8 NIV

(Bettmann/Getty Images)

Rosa Parks with Dr. Martin Luther King Jr. at a dinner in her honor, August 10, 1965.

I believe we all should have people we look up to as examples. I list my husband, Raymond Parks, among the persons I admired most. He was a good man, full of courage and inner strength. Before meeting him, I had never really talked about racial issues with another African-American, outside of my family. And Raymond—"Parks," as I called him—was keenly interested in changing the current racial conditions. Although he had almost no formal schooling, he was very intelligent and read widely.

One thing that really impressed me about Parks was that he refused to be intimidated by white people—unlike many blacks, who figured they had no choice but to stay under "Mr. Charlie's" heel. ("Mr. Charlie" was our name for white men in general.) Parks would have none of it, and he became active in the NAACP and in civil rights issues.

Parks worked courageously for the release of the Scottsboro Boys, a group of nine young black men who were wrongly accused of raping two white women in 1931. They were found guilty and condemned to die for a crime they did not commit. They did not die, thanks to the efforts of many. Anyone who supported them had to meet in secret. To do anything openly for this cause could mean death. And yet Parks, along with the NAACP, fearlessly pursued justice for these men. That is why I later decided to name my legacy after Raymond so that people would know how devoted he was to civil rights and the uplifting of blacks.

My mother, Leona McCauley, helped me to grow up feeling proud of myself and other black people, even while living under racist conditions. She taught me not to judge people by the amount of money they had or the kind of house they lived in or the clothes they wore. People should be judged, she told me, by the respect they have for themselves and others. Her advice helped me to do the hard things that I had to do later in life.

Mother was a woman of determination who believed in reading the Bible for guidance. She also believed in the value of education and saw it as a way to better yourself. She was a schoolteacher and had a teaching certificate, but she did not go to college. Back then black teachers got paid less than white teachers, but the money was better than what housekeepers got. One of the reasons I cofounded, with Elaine Steele, the Rosa and Raymond Parks Institute for Self-Development was because I wanted to carry on what my mother so strongly believed in: the education of our people.

My grandmother, Grandma Rosa, was also dear to me. She helped raise me to be a strong woman. She set an example of caring and love for her children and grandchildren. She was very strong-willed and believed in discipline. I so enjoyed reading the Bible with her. It always made me feel good. I guess that is why it seemed natural for me to read the Bible to her when her eyesight failed. She died when I was sixteen years old. She was calm-spirited and not easily excited. My great-grandmother, Grandma Jane, on the other hand, was excitable and feisty, and Grandpappy would calm her spirit.

My family, and the values they taught me, gave me a sense of who I am. I remember my grandfather, Sylvester Edwards. Because he had very light skin and looked white, he would shake hands with white people and call them by their first names. These acts were extremely risky for a black person to do in those days and could lead to being manhandled or lynched.

Although he looked white, my grandfather was hostile toward

whites. He was not a hateful man; he had simply been cruelly treated by white people all of his life. As a boy he had been beaten, forbidden to have shoes, and starved by the overseer of the plantation he lived on. Too many years of humiliation had given him a belligerent attitude toward white people.

His memory will always be with me. While I do not think I inherited his hostility, my mother and I both learned not to let anyone mistreat us. It was passed down almost in our genes.

Martin Luther King Jr. set a profound example for me in day-to-day living. He was such a young man—just twenty-six years old—when I first met him at the beginning of the bus boycott. I was forty-two.

I'll always remember the way Dr. King would respond to violence. He would use the same words that Jesus said on the cross: "Father, forgive them, for they know not what they do." Brutality was to be received with love, he would say. Though I knew we needed to strive for nonviolence, when I saw the brutal treatment some of us got, I had trouble believing it was always the best thing to do.

Dr. King was a true leader. I never sensed fear in him. I just felt as though he knew what had to be done and took the leading role without regard to consequences. I knew he was destined to do great things. He had an elegance about him and a speaking style that let you know where you stood and inspired you to do the best you could. He truly is a role model for us all. The sacrifice of his life should never be forgotten, and his dream must live on.

During the civil rights movement, another young man came forth to help black people fight the unjust treatment they were receiving. His name was Malcolm X. He was twenty-seven years old. When I look back, this strong-willed man reminded me somewhat of my grandfather. He was full of conviction and pride in his race. The last time I saw him, he was speaking in Detroit, and he signed a program for me.

I admired the way he had changed his position from one of distrust toward whites to one of tolerance and building self-respect among blacks. His ideas were different than what many of us heard publicly, but his strong conviction of self-determination and pride energized blacks in economic development. The way he stood up and voiced himself showed that he was a man to be respected.

During the time that the Reverend Jesse Jackson was running for president, he carried the banner for our people very well. If he continues, I believe he will one day be president. I believe that Reverend Jackson is someone black people can depend on for leadership. I welcomed him as a presidential candidate, and I'll welcome him again if he decides to run. Reverend Jackson made all of us proud during his campaign, and he is continuing to do so today.

Faith

*Trust ye in the L*ORD *for ever: for in the L*ORD
JEHOVAH is everlasting strength.

—ISAIAH 26:4

Rosa Parks speaking at Ebenezer Baptist Church in Atlanta, Georgia, January 1969.

My belief in Christ developed early in life. I was baptized when I was a baby in the African Methodist Episcopal church. In those days, they sprinkled us with water like the Catholics did. I was never pressed, against my will, to go to church—I always wanted to go. I enjoyed dressing up and meeting people. During the service, I paid close attention to the minister's words, the prayer, and the other speakers.

Back then, in the rural South, communities were too poor to support a minister, so the ministers would travel to different places to preach. This was called a circuit. My A.M.E. church met every third Sunday of the month. But on the first, second, and fourth Sundays, we attended services at the Baptist church.

Daily devotions played an important part in my childhood. Every day before supper, and before we went to services on Sundays, my grandmother would read the Bible to me, and my grandfather would pray. We even had devotions before going to pick cotton in the fields. Prayer and the Bible became a part of my everyday thoughts and beliefs. I remember finding such comfort and peace while reading the Bible. Its teachings became a way of life and helped me in dealing with my day-to-day problems.

My favorite book of the Bible is Psalms. I turn there for strength when I am bothered. The words are so poetic and full of meaning for me. In one of the darkest moments of my life—when I was eighteen—I needed help, and I went to Psalm 27:1–7. My mother used to read it to me when I was a child:

> The LORD is my light and my salvation;
>> whom shall I fear?
> The LORD is the strength of my life;
>> of whom shall I be afraid?
> When the wicked, even mine enemies and my foes,
>> came upon me to eat up my flesh,
>> they stumbled and fell.
> Though an host should encamp against me,
>> my heart shall not fear;
> Though war should rise against me,
>> in this will I be confident.
> One thing I have desired of the LORD,
>> that will I seek after:
> That I may dwell in the house of the LORD
>> all the days of my life,
>> to behold the beauty of the LORD,
>> and to inquire in his temple.

For in the time of trouble
>   he shall hide me in his pavilion;
in the secret of his tabernacle shall he hide me;
>   he shall set me up upon a rock.
And now shall mine head be lifted up
>   above mine enemies round about me.
Therefore will I offer in his tabernacle sacrifices of joy;
>   I will sing, yea, I will sing praises unto the Lord.
Hear, O Lord, when I cry with my voice.

The message from this Scripture does not fade with time. I read it over and over again when my spirits are down. I am thankful to my mother, grandfather, and grandmother for bringing me closer to God by making the Bible a part of my life early on.

I have problems just like everyone else. Whenever I do, I think about my grandmother and my mother. They were such strong women, who always taught me to place my faith in God and to read the Bible.

I remember when I got married, I stopped reading the Bible.

When my mother found out that I had stopped, she told me that one should not stop reading the Bible; there was always something new to learn by reading it. On that day, I started back reading the Bible and have not stopped since.

The Bible is such a source of strength for me that it is hard to say which Scripture I look at for any one thing. But when I feel discouraged, I read Psalm 23 to restore my soul:

> The Lord is my shepherd;
>> I shall not want.
> He maketh me to lie down in green pastures;
>> he leadeth me beside the still waters.
> He restoreth my soul;
>> he leadeth me in the paths of righteousness
>> for his name's sake.
> Yea, though I walk through the valley
>> of the shadow of death,
> I will fear no evil;
>> for thou art with me;
>> thy rod and thy staff, they comfort me.
> Thou preparest a table before me
>> in the presence of mine enemies;
> thou anointest my head with oil;

my cup runneth over.
Surely goodness and mercy shall follow me
all the days of my life;
and I will dwell in the house of the Lord
for ever.

During the civil rights movement, we were troubled by hatred. We would pray a lot. One thing we used to keep us going was the moving words of certain hymns, many of which had been passed down from the slave days. They gave us a sense of togetherness with our people. Singing gave us the feeling that—with God's help—we could overcome whatever we were facing.

One of my favorite hymns is "Woke Up This Morning with My Mind Stayed on Jesus." We would sing, "Woke Up This Morning with My Mind on Freedom." Another is "I Am Bound for the Promised Land." Often we would substitute the word "freedom" for a key word of the hymn. For instance, we'd sing:

> *CHORUS:*
> *I am bound for the freedom land,*
> *I am bound for the freedom land*

O who will come and go with me?
I am bound for the freedom land.
On Jordan's stormy banks I stand,
And cast a wishful eye;
To Canaan's fair and freedom land,
Where my possessions lie.
(CHORUS)
All o'er those wide extended plains
Shines one eternal day;
There God the Son forever reigns,
And scatters night away.
(CHORUS)
No chilling winds, nor poisonous breath
Can reach that healthful shore;
Sickness and sorrow, pain and death,
Are felt and feared no more.
(CHORUS)
When shall I reach that happy place,
And be forever blest?
When shall I see my Father's face,
And in his bosom rest?
(CHORUS)
Filled with delight, my raptured soul

Would here no longer stay;
Tho' Jordan's waves around me roll,
Fearless I'd launch away.

These moving songs gave us the strength to keep our dreams of true freedom alive. Whenever we sang them, we knew there would be no turning back.

Values

Train up a child in the way he should go: and
when he is old, he will not depart from it.

—PROVERBS 22:6

Rosa Parks in front of the mural at Dexter Avenue Martin
Luther King Memorial Church, November 21, 1992.

Even though blacks were treated as second-class citizens without many rights, my mother used to always tell me that all of God's children were supposed to be free. She kept telling me this over and over again until I truly felt that one day we would be free, because God had meant for it to be this way. So my belief in freedom goes way back to the days when my mother used to sing "O Freedom Over Me." I will never forget those words:

O freedom
O freedom
O freedom over me
And before I'd be a slave
I'd be buried in my grave
And go home to my Lord and be free.

O weeping
O weeping
O weeping over me
And before I'd be a slave
I'd be buried in my grave
And go home to my Lord and be free.

O crying
O crying

O crying over me
And before I'd be a slave
I'd be buried in my grave
And go home to my Lord and be free.

No injustice
No injustice
No injustice over me
And before I'd be a slave
I'd be buried in my grave
And go home to my Lord and be free.

These words formed my feelings about being free. They gave me strength when things seemed bad, and they guided my thoughts about what I was willing to do to be free. So when I declined to give up my seat, it was not that day or that bus in particular. I just wanted to be free like everybody else. I did not want to be continually humiliated over something I had no control over: the color of my skin.

I am troubled by all the racism and violence in our society; there is still too much of it today. What troubles me is that so many young people, including college students, have come out for white supremacy. More and more incidents of racial violence on college campuses have occurred as a result of the white-supremacy form of thinking. We still have a long way to go. I try to keep hope alive. It is better to teach—and live—equality and love than it is to teach hatred. I would like to see everyone living together in peace, harmony, and love, not dwelling on the horrors of the past. It is time to move forward.

The Martin Luther King Jr. holiday reflects values and ideas that benefit all of us—not only black people. It is unfortunate there was so much trouble getting it approved a few years back. Now that it has passed, I hope it will help to bring about the ideals of Dr. King—and of all Christians—for the good of our people and for the good of the whole world.

Quiet Strength

In quietness and in confidence shall be your strength.

—ISAIAH 30:15

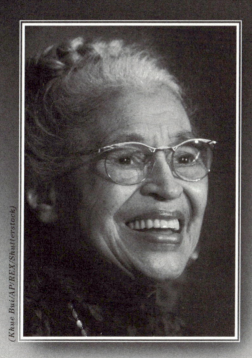

Rosa Parks

Many ask whether I am discouraged in the struggle for justice, peace, and harmony. My answer has always been no. People will need help whenever and wherever they are oppressed. As long as any effort is being made to help others, I will not allow myself to be discouraged. I prefer to have a positive attitude and focus on positive ideals. If you let yourself become discouraged, then you do not have much to look forward to.

My strength has always come from the church. I have always gained strength from thinking about the Bible and from the faith of my family. Church has always been a place where we can turn to God for rest and encouragement. It lifts the spirit and helps us to go on. Wherever I travel, I try to attend a church service.

Perhaps my only "secret" is my attitude toward life. Because I have such high ideals, I feel strongly when they are violated in the world around me. I do not like to see people treated in a way

I would not want to be treated. Whenever I see this happening, I do everything in my power to help the cause.

People all over the world need help. There is still famine in Somalia, war in the Middle East, the ruins of apartheid in South Africa, and many other places of conflict. As long as the civilized world allows inhuman treatment to be inflicted upon any people, then our freedom is threatened as well.

I have traveled many roads since the Montgomery bus-boycott days. Each day along the way has given me a sense of pride in who I am. On many occasions I was tested, and I had to find my way through a maze of choices and options. But I refused to go along with the unfair rules. Back in the segregation days, when I went downtown, I walked up and down the stairs rather than ride the elevators marked "colored." Often I walked a mile from home to work and then back again rather than ride the bus, because the buses were the worst of the options. On hot days when my throat was dry, I walked past the water fountains marked "colored" and waited until I got wherever I was going to get something to drink. I have never allowed myself to be treated as a second-class citizen. You must respect yourself before others can respect you.

There is work to do; that is why I cannot stop or sit still. As long as a child needs help, as long as people are not free, there will be work to do. As long as an elderly person is attacked or in need of support, there is work to do. As long as we have bigotry and crime, we have work to do. This is why I think it is important to tell my story. We have come so far since the days of segregation, but there is always something to do to make things better. All human beings should have equal opportunities.

Determination

*Be ye steadfast, unmovable, always abounding
in the work of the Lord.*

—1 CORINTHIANS 15:58

Rosa Parks with the Reverend Joseph Lowery in front of
Martin Luther King Jr.'s tomb, Atlanta, July 3, 1989.

When I retired from Congressman John Conyers' office in 1988, I never thought of leaving that job as a retirement from life. I just felt that I now had more time to do more of my work for the people. Many people felt that I deserved a rest and that I should slow down. I informed them that I was not going to be idle by any means. I do not know how to slow down. I hope to expand my activities. I will continue to move on at whatever pace I can.

School has always been important to me, and from the earliest time that I knew my mother was a teacher, I wanted to go. She would not let me go right away, though, because I was small for my age and sick a lot. I got very upset about that until finally I was able to go to school.

I very much wanted to continue my high school education when I was younger. But circumstances made it unlikely at the time. At one point my grandmother became ill, and I could not return to school. Later my mother became ill when I was going to attend the high school connected with Alabama State Teachers' College. I chose to take care of her while my brother worked. To me it was more important to take care of them.

They were very dear to me. Sometimes one must make painful choices, but we must think of others as well. I did not give up on my dream, though. Later, with my husband Raymond's support, I received my high school diploma in 1934.

For many years, I had wanted to start an organization to help young people. In 1987, along with Elaine Steele, I cofounded the Rosa and Raymond Parks Institute for Self-Development. Together we began a variety of programs that will help Detroit youth to pursue their education and create a promising future for themselves. I see it as a way of giving back to my people.

Today's youth have such great potential, and I want to help them develop marketable skills that will enable them to reach that potential. The institute offers scholarships for motivated young people and provides courses in communication and economic skills and in political and health awareness. Education of this kind, I believe, will make it possible for them to have a sense of hope, dignity, and pride. I do not see the activity of helping young people as work but as something that must be done. I have always felt a need to work with youth. I will not give up on them.

I have been working since before I was twelve years old. I never worked because I enjoyed it but because it was necessary. Now there is new work to do. As I recall the history of racism over the past generations, it brings back memories I would rather forget. But since I cannot forget them, I try to use them to bring about change. By traveling the country and talking about civil rights history, I am not living in the past. I am fighting for more justice. I will keep struggling for freedom and equality as long as I have the strength.

It is important to keep yourself grounded in faith. When things are not going the way you want, you must keep hope alive that things will get better. When I refused to give up my seat, I had no idea what it would spark or what change would result. I simply did it because I thought nobody else would do anything. I was grateful that the act inspired others to unify in the pursuit of justice.

Youth

Tell it to your children,
and let your children tell it to their children,
and their children to the next generation.

—JOEL 1:3 NIV

Rosa parks signs autographs for children in 1991.

I am motivated and inspired by young people and children. My eyes light up whenever children come around. They are our future. If the changes we began in the civil rights movement are going to continue, they will be the ones who have to do it.

The world is not the same as in my early life, but young people still have serious problems they must face in today's society. They have to adjust so much more quickly to a fast-paced lifestyle. I do not think they are really that much different than in my day, but they do have many more distractions, such as video games, MTV, and greater peer pressure.

I remember, as a girl, the run-ins I had with white children. In most cases, they just called me names, but some were much worse. It was not that the white kids meant to be cruel, but they had been indoctrinated with those types of attitudes by the adults around them. It is important for us to bring up our youngsters in homes without prejudice and hatred.

Too many of today's youths do not know who they are or where they have been. And as a result, they do not know where they are going. Too many are not staying in school and taking advantage of the opportunities a good education can provide.

They are not motivated to learn what is necessary to be good citizens, get good jobs, or start their own businesses. There is nothing wrong with these young people. We must help them. It is our job to show them the way, to teach them values, to prepare them for the future, and to help them set goals.

One thing we need to do is tell young people about our struggles for civil rights. I think they sometimes have difficulty separating fact from fiction when it comes to our history. It's important that they hear how things were and what some of us had to go through before them. Many of them do not appreciate the suffering their ancestors have endured to bring them the degree of freedom they now enjoy. They must be reminded that many people have died so that they can have what they have now.

Racism is still alive and will stay with us as long as we allow it. But we can teach our youth to continue the effort and not lose the gains we have achieved. We can show them how opportunities come along and how individuals today can still bring about change.

We must teach children to prepare for the future—how to set goals for their lives and for their careers. We must do more to inspire, train, and motivate them. They need effective role models to help them develop strength of character. They should be taught to understand the difference between knowledge, feeling, and behaviour. Rather than be so hard on them, we should instead set an example for them to follow. Here are seven key areas we can use:

1. Treating all youth with love and respect, setting good examples for them, supporting social behavior and correcting negative behavior.
2. Helping all young people to know one another as persons and to respect and care about one another.
3. Teaching values by using the rich content of history, literature, and the Bible.
4. Showing young people how to develop the ability to work hard and to do the best that they can do.
5. Encouraging youth to work together so they can see the value of cooperating with others for a common good.
6. Guiding young people in experiences that show them how to solve problems without conflict and force.
7. Providing opportunities for youth to perform school, home, and community services.

If we can set the example in our homes and communities, we can save our children. I have faith in what the good people of this country have done in the past and can do today.

What message would I have for young people today—of any race? Work hard, do not be discouraged, and in everything you do, try to make our country—and the world—a better place for us all. You are among my treasured friends and this country's most treasured possessions. You are our future. I see your energy as a real force for change. But you must know who you are, where you are, and where you have been so that you will know where you are going. Once you know this, then you will be on the pathway to freedom.

Do not forget to exercise self-control, nurture your spiritual life, and remain health-conscious. Stay away from drugs and alcohol, or else your mind and body will not be free. And remember: no matter what the circumstances are, it is best to pursue behavior that is above reproach, because then you will be respected for your actions.

The Future

Where there is no vision, the people perish.

—PROVERBS 29:18

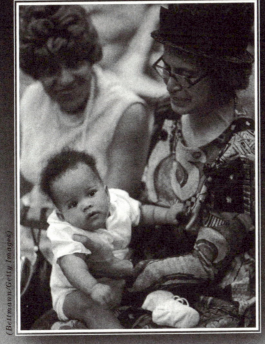

(Bettmann/Getty Images)

Rosa Parks at Detroit's Black Expo 1972. The child's name is Afriye Amerson.
In Ghanian language, the name "Afriye" means "born at the right time."

I want to be remembered as a person who stood up to injustice, who wanted a better world for young people; and most of all, I want to be remembered as a person who wanted to be free and wanted others to be free. And my fight will continue as long as people are being oppressed.

Looking back on that December day in 1955, I feel proud of the progress we have made. The number of black mayors in this country has soared from six to more than three hundred. Black elected officials have increased from three hundred to five thousand. But we still have many differences to reconcile. I would like to see us put the past behind us and live in peace and harmony. We must all work toward being free.

I have been truly blessed over the years. And I'm very thankful that I have been spared to see this day. I am always grateful for each day God has given me. I have learned that, in order to bring about change, one must take the first step, or else it will not be done.

Despite our gains, discrimination is still very much at work in this country. Despite the efforts of those committed to bringing about social justice in America, barriers to equal opportunity have not been broken down. But that has not caused me to become discouraged. We need to continue the struggle to realize our goal of equality. The dream of which Dr. King spoke—one that should be held by all—has yet to be realized. So the movement continues.

Back in the days of segregation, we did not have any of what they called "civil rights." All we could do was try to survive from one day to the next. Today we have a modern civil rights movement. We must keep it alive. I am still hopeful for progress. I think positive.

It is important that people do not become comfortable with the gains we have made in the last forty years. Things have gotten better, but our freedom is threatened every time one of our young people is killed by another child, every time an elderly person is violated in his or her home, every time a person gets stopped and beaten by the police because of the color of their skin. Until these wrongs and others are dealt with, the movement must live on.

I still believe there can be a day when we will have true freedom: a day when people "will not be judged by the color of their skin but by the content of their character," to quote Dr. King. We must consider a day when we can all get along regardless of our race. This is not a dream. It is alive within the ability of us all.

My message to the world is that we must come together and live as one. There is only one world; and yet we, as a people, have treated the world as if it were divided. We cannot allow the gains we have made to erode. Although we have a long way to go, I do believe that we can achieve Dr. King's dream of a better world.

From time to time I catch glimpses of that world. I can see a world where children do not learn hatred in their homes. I can see a world where mothers and fathers have the last and most important word.

I can see a world in which one respects the rights of one's neighbors. I can see a world in which all adults protect the innocence of children.

I can see a world in which people do not call each other names based on skin color. I can see a world free of acts of violence. I can see a world in which people of all races and all religions work together to improve the quality of life for everyone.

I can see this world because it exists today in small pockets of this country and in a small pocket of every person's heart. If we will look to God and work together—not only here but everywhere—then others will see this world too and help to make it a reality.

Epilogue

By Gregory J. Reed, Esq.

There is a time for everything,
and a season for every activity.

ECCLESIASTES 3:1 NIV

On October 24, 2005, America lost a great hero, my friend and client Mrs. Rosa Parks. Her death and the shining example of her life caused an outpouring of emotion and national mourning. I will never forget the indelible words she wrote to me on June 18, 1995, "You have improved my welfare more than I could have imagined. I believe the Lord is guiding your path. I feel comforted and protected knowing that. Spend as much time with your young daughters [Arian and Ashley] as you can. You are a great role model. Love, Rosa Parks."

Starting in 1955, Rosa played a vital role during the civil rights movement. She placed her life in danger and bravely confronted segregation. Yet by the 1980s her legacy had faded from cultural memory.

My path first crossed with Mrs. Rosa Parks in 1987. I was in the midst of launching my fourth play, *MLK: We Are the Dream*, as part of the movement to establish the Martin Luther King Jr. Day holiday. Unfortunately, publicity for the play was gaining little traction. The community's lukewarm response demonstrated how the civil rights movement had lost its luster and value among the new generation of young African Americans and whites. I contacted radio talk show host and Detroit-based community activist Joe Madison for help. In our brief meeting, Joe mentioned that Mrs. Parks's car had been totaled in a traffic accident and she was taking the bus again to get around. I told Joe, "We will use the play proceeds to buy Mrs. Parks a new car."

The first stop of the play's five-city tour was at the Detroit Music Hall and was nearly sold out. It is forever engraved in my mind—the intensified energy at the close of the play, the room buzzing, the community excited as Joe and I stepped out on the stage. The backstage curtain was lifted to show Mrs. Parks's new, red Buick automobile. The audience cheered, shouted, and clapped, happy to participate in giving back to the mother of the civil rights movement.

That event was an eye-opener for me as to why it is so

important to preserve the legacies of our historical figures for future generations. For the next three years, I prayed to be able to legally represent Mrs. Parks.

My path crossed with Mrs. Parks again in 1990. She had since lost her husband, her brother, and her mother and was determined to find legal support. After speaking to a friend of my sister Sharon, Mrs. Parks walked into my office and said, "I'd like for you to be my lawyer." I smiled and was overwhelmed by the honor.

It became a personal goal of mine to support Mrs. Parks's legacy and seek national acknowledgement for her world-changing efforts. I compiled a list of twenty-seven goals we could work toward that would resurrect her image and ensure that her tireless efforts were honored and recognized. Among the list of notable goals were the Presidential Medal of Freedom Award, Congressional Gold Medal, a statue, a museum, a postal stamp, and a book in her own words. I reviewed the list with Mrs. Parks and she said, "No one has ever done this for me before." Through the Rosa Parks Legacy nonprofit, we accomplished twenty-six of the twenty-seven goals, all on a nonexistent budget and in a ten-year span.

Hired by Mrs. Parks, I assembled a legal defense team of attorneys—Johnnie L. Cochran Jr., Stephanie Hammonds, and

Richard Manson—to protect the usage of the Rosa Parks name. We played a key role in the U. S. Supreme Court decision, settling the 2005 lawsuit against BMG music company and the rap duo OutKast.

On August 30, 1994, an intruder entered Mrs. Parks's home, physically assaulted her, and took her money. The incident shocked and embarrassed American citizens. I was horrified and sought to help in any way I could.

Though the attack was a dark, horrendous moment, it led to a spiritual light and inspired renewed interest in her story. Zondervan, a Christian publishing house, reached out, offering a blank contract to publish a book with Mrs. Rosa Parks. This book, originally titled *Quiet Strength*, was first released in January 1995 as a result of writing for forty days and nights in our efforts to resurrect her legacy. After a dark moment in her life, this book served as a source of joy and light in Mrs. Parks's life. During the book tour, lines of people wanting to talk to and touch Mrs. Parks wrapped around several city blocks. I witnessed people in lines: fainting, crying, and overcome by emotion as they approached this legendary woman.

In honor of Mrs. Parks, an unprecedented tribute album was created by Verity Records as a companion to the book. Arranged by CEO Barry Weiss, the album included songs from 100 elite musicians such as Yolanda Adams, Oleta Adams, Vanessa Bell Armstrong, and Fred Hammonds.

In 1996, Mrs. Rosa Parks was awarded the Presidential Medal of Freedom. In 1999, she received the Congressional Gold Medal and *Time* magazine heralded Mrs. Parks as one of the most influential and iconic figures of the twentieth century. Mrs. Parks's long-time friend Elaine Steele and myself negotiated and cofounded the The Rosa Parks Museum in Montgomery, Alabama, located at the site of her arrest. The museum is still one of the state's major tourist attractions.

Mrs. Parks received more mail than ever which led us to coauthor a second book, *Dear Mrs. Parks: A Dialogue with Today's Youth,* published in 1997. And Mrs. Parks received Michigan's first NAACP Image Award for Outstanding Literature.

Recognized as an international icon and inspirational hero, Mrs. Rosa Parks passed away at age ninety-two on October 24, 2005. Mrs. Parks was the first African American woman to lie in state in the United States Capitol rotunda. Her life was honored with memorial services arranged by ONeil D. Swanson in Montgomery; Washington, DC; and Detroit. The story of her courageous act is told in museums and schools internationally. The legacy of her dignity of character and her quiet strength to defend the rights of others continues to inspire the nation today.

"The woman we honored today held no public office, she wasn't a wealthy woman, didn't appear in the society pages. And yet when the history of this country is written, it is this small, quiet woman whose name will be remembered long after the names of senators and presidents have been forgotten."

—U. S. SENATOR BARACK OBAMA,

ROSA PARKS'S FUNERAL SERVICE

Rosa Parks: A Chronology

1913   Born in Tuskegee, Alabama, on February 4.

1924   Enters school in Montgomery, Alabama.

1929   Leaves school to care for grandmother.

1932   Marries Raymond Parks in Pine Level, Alabama.

1934   Receives high school diploma.

1943   Becomes secretary of the Montgomery NAACP.

1943   Tries to register to vote and is denied.

1943   Is forced off bus for not entering at the back door.

1944   Is again denied the opportunity to register to vote.

1945   Finally receives certificate for voting.

1949   Becomes adviser to the NAACP Youth Council.

1955   Meets the Reverend Martin Luther King Jr.

1955   Is arrested on December 1 for not yielding her seat to a white man on a Montgomery bus.

1955   Stands trial and is found guilty on December 5. Montgomery bus boycott begins.

1956   Loses job at Montgomery Fair department store in
       January.

1957   Moves to Detroit.

1963   Attends civil rights march on Washington.

1965   Participates in Selma-to-Montgomery civil rights
       march. Begins working for Congressman John Conyers
       in Detroit.

1977   Husband, Raymond Parks, dies. Sylvester McCauley,
       brother, dies.

1979   Mother, Leona McCauley, dies.

1987   Cofounds the Rosa and Raymond Parks Institute for
       Self-Development, with Elaine Steele.

1991   Bust of Rosa Parks is unveiled at Smithsonian
       Institution, Washington, D.C.

1992   Meets Dr. Daisaku Ikeda, founder and president of
       Soka Gakkai International.

1992   Publishes her first book, *Rosa Parks: My Story* (New
       York: Dial Books) with Jim Haskins.

1994   Trip to Japan; receives honorary doctorate degree/
       Soka University.

1994   Trip to Stockholm, Sweden, to receive Rosa Parks
       Peace Prize and light the Peace Candle.

1995   Fortieth anniversary, Montgomery bus boycott.

1995   *Quiet Strength,* coauthored with Gregory J. Reed.

1995   Parks Legacy non-profit formed to address intellec-
tual property and authorization of using the Rosa
Parks name.

1995   Tribute album released, including contributions from
100 elite gospel artists.

1995   Sarah's Attic creates Rosa Parks figurines.

1995   Addresses audience at the U.S. Capitol during the
Million Man March.

1996   Presidential Medal of Freedom awarded by President
Bill Clinton.

1997   Nationwide "Think Different" campaign by Apple Inc.
features Rosa Parks.

1997   *Dear Mrs. Parks; A Dialogue with Todays Youth* is
published.

1998   *Secrets of Inner Power; A Profile in Courage*
coauthored by Rosa Parks and Deepak Chopra and produced by Gregory J. Reed.

1999   Julia Carson, inspired by reading *Quiet Strength,*
awards Rosa Parks the Congressional Gold Medal.

1999   Rosa Parks *Quiet Strength* Commemorative coin
issued by U.S. Mint.

1999   Files lawsuit to protect the usage of her name against

BMG Records and rapper duo OutKast, U. S. Federal
Court denies Mrs. Parks.

2000   Rosa Parks Museum founded at Troy State University
in Montgomery, Alabama.

2000   *Rosa Parks; A Life* by Douglas Brinkley authorized by
Rosa Parks and published.

2001   *Rosa Parks; More Than a Bus Story* play by Von
Washington.

2001   U.S. Court of Appeals rules Parks has a right to the
usage of her name, BMG appeals to Supreme Court.

2002   *The Rosa Parks Story* movie, featuring Angela
Bassett.

2005   Parks settles with BMG and OutKast after Supreme
Court ruling.

2005   Dies of natural causes on October 24, 2005.

2008   *Dear Mr. Mandela, Dear Mrs. Parks*: *Children's
Letters, Global Lessons* exhibit first opens at the
Nelson Mandela National Museum in South Africa,
sponsored by the Department of State Bureau of
Education and Cultural Affairs.

2013   Rosa Parks postal stamp released during the cele-
bration of Rosa Parks's 100th birthday.

2014   An asteroid, Rosaparks, named in her honor.

2015   Rosa Parks Railway Station opens in Paris.

2016   Rosa Parks's niece purchases Rosa Parks's house in
        Detroit for $500 and donates the building to the artist
        Ryan Mendoza.

—About the Coauthor—

Gregory J. Reed is a prominent attorney representing notable persons and subject-matters of distinction in the United States. His contributions carry national and international significance. The author of sixteen books including various bestsellers and editions translated in German and Japanese, Reed is a multi-NAACP Image award winner. His multiple outstanding literature awards includes the first American Book Award in Michigan for *Economic Empowerment through the Church*, presented to Congress in 1994. *Quiet Strength* inspired the Congressional Gold Medal presented to Mrs. Rosa Parks by Hon. Julia Carson. Reed has been honored by President Obama for his writings and work for Rosa Parks. *Quiet Strength* was the first book accompanied by a tribute album including contributions from 100 elite gospel artists and produced by Reed.